This book is all about building your little one's hair confidence, imagination and inspiring the superhero inside of her.

I hope that every little girl coloring these pages never forgets her hair will always be her crown and glory.

MY HAIR IS NATURAL.
I WAS BORN LIKE THIS.

MY HAIR IS LONG. IT GROWS FROM MY HEAD.

MY HAIR IS SHORT. IT MAKES ME FEEL SUPER CUTE.

MY HAIR IS FULL OF CURLS. IT'S BOUNCY, JUST LIKE ME !

MY HAIR IS BIG AND BEAUTIFUL.

MY HAIR IS BRAIDED. IT DOES SPECIAL THINGS.

MY HAIR IS PUFFY. THAT'S MY SUPERGIRL POWER!

MY HAIR IS THICK. IT HOLDS ALL OF MY TREASURE.

MY HAIR IS
SPECIAL.

MY HAIR IS MY CROWN AND GLORY.

NOW IT'S YOUR TURN. DRAW A PICTURE OF YOUR BEAUTIFUL HAIR.

I hope your little one

enjoyed this book.

If you have any feedback for me

then, I'd love to hear from you.

Email me at tqmccall@gmail.com